The dream for humanization, whose concretization is always process, always becoming, goes through rupture with real, concrete ties of an economic order, a political one, social, ideological, etc., which are dooming us to dehumanization. Dreaming is, therefore, a requirement or a condition, which has become permanent in the history we make and which makes and re-makes us.
(Paulo Freire, Daring to Dream: Toward a Pedagogy of the Unfinished, 2007: ix)

Dream Builders University's

SEVEN AREAS OF PARENTAL INFLUENCE

CONFIDENCE

CREATIVITY

CONNECTIVITY

TRUST

INTEREST

ACCEPTANCE

LEGACY

"I dedicate this book to the many adults that have blessed me with their parenting. My parents, grandparents, aunts, mentors...I am who I am because of what you all have poured into me. Because of you I can dream!"

--L. Kobie Wilkerson

"Thank you to my parents (Dornessa Ward-Shipp and Willie Shipp) and all of the other adults who are a part of my village, the village that raised me up to be the man I am today. Because I love you so much I will list you all. Thank you Eric Thomas, Chris Nelms, Mike Smith, Ozzie Davis, Kim and Mark Fowler, Buddy LaRosa, Ms. Jackson, Lora Ward, Dr. Earlena Wilson, Tyrone Ward, George Spencer, Thomas Stewart, Vincent Ward, Jeff Kitchen, Pauline Bley, Luis Perez, Eddie Trice, Rodney Ringer, Elvin Ward Sr., Paul Simmering, Joe Albert Sr., Charlie Long and Carol Beirne. All of you have made such a profound impact with your love, encouragement and direction in my life. In this book is a small portion of my personal struggle and your efforts counting in the life of the young man you invested in.

I LOVE YOU and know that because of you the world is a better place because of what you have done for me."

--Your son, LaMarqué D. Ward Sr., M. Ed.

FROM LAMARQUÉ & L. KOBIE

Thank you for taking the time to read this booklet. Over the last combined 30 years of working in youth development and education, we have made some very sharp observations about relational patterns between parents and children. In these relationships, we have seen parents who provide physically with possessions, but struggle to provide spiritually and emotionally, and we have also seen parents who struggle to provide basic needs, but provide support and encouragement to their children and their children do great things. Regardless of if you find yourself at either end of these extremes, or in the middle, we have come to recognize there is a fine balance each parent has to find with their children in order to achieve meaningful success. In this booklet, we would like to explore and share a relational pattern that has shown promise and success with parents and students.

Dream Building for Parents is a principle driven framework that provides parents with a fresh perspective and new ideas on how to encourage their children in positive ways to pursue their purpose, while intentionally extracting their child's full potential. One idea we have discovered is being the message you bring. You have to model the behavior you expect from your children. As we all know, actions speak a great deal louder than words. We have come to realize that children are more apt to listen to what you do, and just watch what you say. The greatest things you will ever say to them will speak through your actions.

LAMARQUÉ

As a parent of six, I noticed that my children were taking on some of my negative attributes. I had to take out my Michael Jackson song and start with the "Man in the Mirror." As I began working on my character and modeling different characteristics, my children, wife, and family noticed a difference in me. Being consistent in these areas earned me trust and respect inside and outside of my home. Only then could I hold my family accountable in these same areas – and it was received graciously. Being willing to be transparent and admit that I was participating in the lifelong learning process was important as well. When they saw the change and willingness in me to be open about my flaws, they began to take the journey with me—this is the most challenging part of this booklet.

All positions in life are temporary. You have the power to choose every day to improve your position or allow it to go downward.
                                                            - Frank Accoin

I use this quote because if you're not where you want to be, it's okay. We're all striving to be better, but we have to be aware of what needs to be improved. What a shame to live a life and never reach your full potential because of things you were never made aware of. What's even worse is it impacts our children and possibly their children for generations. If someone doesn't challenge these ideas and habits, the cycle is NEVER broken.

Is it easy? No. During this process, my children shared their thoughts with me without restraint. Ouch! They shared how they viewed the life I lived in front of them. At that point I knew how to win them over and give them a voice to address real life issues. Now, they help solve problems and always bring input to the table.

Did I change? Absolutely. I learned exactly what was needed, and figured out what had to be eliminated in order for me to receive it in real time. Yes, I want my children to listen to me and do well in school, but I had to be a model of my own advice first.

L. KOBIE

As a fairly new parent I was always told, "Yeah you teach kids and you say you love them like they are your own, but wait till you have your own child, you'll see." Well, I have my own and I promise you what I am seeking to instill in her is exactly the same things I sought to instill in my students. The only difference is no one is coming to pick her up.

What I have realized in doing extensive reading, research, simply living, and presenting to 1000's of teachers (who many happen to be parents) is the key to getting children to achieve ALL we want them to be is to first be ALL that we desire to be. Sounds simple doesn't it? But as the Puerto Rican proverb states "There is a GREAT distance between said and done."

This framework, if followed, is going to cost you something. We don't promise it will be easy. Actually, it will be challenging and at times really frustrating. What we do promise is that if you take the journey, and use the framework, you will not only become a better parent, but you will also become a better and a bigger person in the process. I live by this quote: "Without continuous self-development you are right now all that you will ever become. The real hell begins when you meet the you that you could've been." We wrote this book in order to help you help your children achieve their dreams, so they will never have to run into the person they "could've been." Because of you, they will be successfully on the journey to becoming all they are destined to be.

New Term Alert!

Unintended Family: A family that is the product of an intimate relationship between two people. Neither party intended to create a child or children but have them. The entire family is left holding the emotional baggage and struggling to pick up the pieces.

DREAM BUILDING FOR PARENTS

WHAT IS DREAM BUILDING?

Dream Building is recognizing a desired vision or goal and following through with precise action steps to make the vision/dream or goal a reality.

WHAT IS DREAM BUILDING FOR PARENTS?

Dream Building for Parents is a relational and coaching framework to support children in achieving their dreams. This relationship is reciprocal in nature, so as the child shares with you they also come to learn more about you. The parents are learning from their child, adjusting and encouraging them to take ownership of the precise action steps that will make their vision/dream a reality. We believe children learn from us, but the majority of this process is the parent learning from them.

Dream Building for Parents is partially academic and instructional, but the majority is visual. Our kids model us. They literally see us as bigger versions of themselves. It is for that reason Dream Building has to be a universal language—it must be seen, heard, spoken and experienced. The principles have to be lived out in the home, on the job, with friends, with your spouse or significant other, with family, etc. The best part is it does not matter what social class you are in, where you are now, or where you have come from. Desire, discipline, and life ownership brings a reward to anyone who lives life directed with those principles.

So, yes—there has to be conversations, but the best conversation must be spoken through your lifestyle. There has to be a culture of progress and hope. Embracing this concept will challenge you to revisit your core values (We told you it wasn't going to be easy). What we have discovered is that EVERY family has principles or values that guide their lives (whether they know them or not). Some of them are more positive than others, but they are there. What hasn't happened is that as a family they have not been intentionally acknowledged and written down. You may have had this talk already but have not talked about it in the home in a while. Start talking about it and get it written down, and maybe even hang it on a wall. Then you can inspect what you expect.

This is what we want you to get out of this book:

7 Areas of Parental Influence
Family exercises
The Pyramid of Achievement
Practical life wisdom

Here is an exercise that you can do with your family before you even read the book. Complete it yourself first, then do it with your kids—allowing them to complete their answers on their own. You want to see what has been internalized. You want the raw data of what their reality is. Simply ask them the questions. If they are old enough have them write their answers down. We promise this will be a telling experience for you.

What do you believe about your family's vision, faith, and legacy?

_____
_____
_____
_____
_____
_____
_____
_____
_____
_____

What do you believe about education?

_____
_____
_____
_____

_____
_____
_____
_____

What do you believe about your faith?

_____
_____
_____
_____
_____
_____
_____
_____

What do you like most about being a part of your family?

_____
_____
_____
_____
_____
_____
_____
_____

What do you like least about being a part of your family?

_____
_____
_____
_____
_____
_____
_____
_____

The Pyramid of Achievement

The diagram below embodies the support and direction we believe all children need.

Parents are the foundation to achievement and success for life. The pastor/rabbi and mentor/coach act as guardrails. Parents provide the foundation that children need to be creative in designing their life, but parents must enlist others who will serve as surrogates. These people could be church leaders, uncles or aunts, youth coaches, or mentors. This is essential to the growth and development in your child's life. It also creates accountability when they aren't home with you. It's also very essential that your children have other people who have your permission to hold them accountable. We call that twice as much love.

It takes a village to raise one child. – African Proverb

Even though many young people may act like they don't want boundaries, they really do. We have spoken to hundreds of young people who wish their parents were more their parents and not friends. They have made a lot of life mistakes and realized down the road that their parents did not give them firm direction when needed. Our goal is to help curb and minimize these stories. We tell them: you can't turn back the hands of time, but you can make a choice today to start building your dream by taking ownership of the disciplines that will open the doors to the life you desire.

Young people are like lions; they will bite you for two reasons: they are starving or they've been provoked. We would rather inspire them to greatness versus provoking them. We wouldn't want them to bite us when they're starved for attention, direction, or assurance. When we watch the news and read the newspaper, it's all over the place. Our children are young lions and they are roaring loud and clear. Can we hear them? As we write for students, parents, and teachers, it's our hope that we can begin to uplift students in a draft of personal growth, hope, and unleashed potential.

PYRAMID OF ACHIEVEMENT

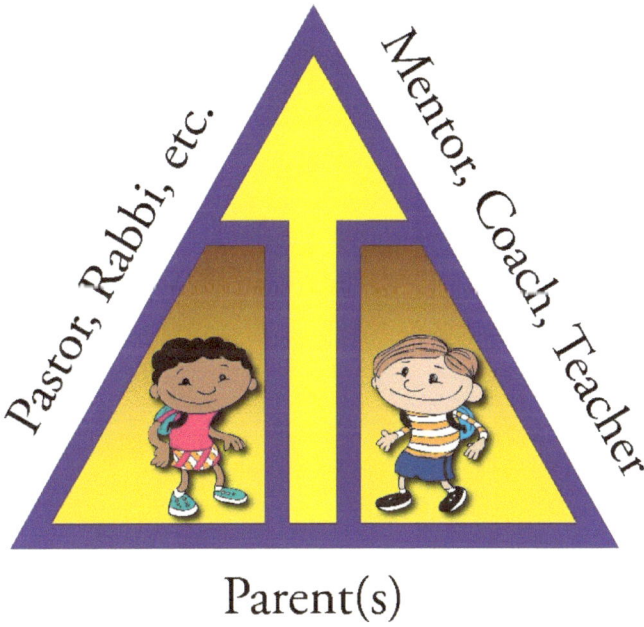

DREAM BUILDING AS A PARENT

Parents work hard every day to provide food, clothes, and shelter for their family. It feels good, but parenting is more than just providing the basic needs, buying clothes, taking vacations, and allowing them to play sports. Living life gets busy. If you don't intentionally pause and take inventory, you'll look up and the time you should have taken to instill and create a solid foundation will be gone. As parents ourselves, we've experienced some of these same obstacles as well. As a result, we created and incorporated the 7 Areas of Parental Influence. We thought of areas where we could challenge ourselves to be better parents—to build a better relationship with our children and help breathe life into their dreams.

In this booklet we share the mistakes we have made, knowledge we've learned, and the wisdom to connect as a parent with children. We don't want to tell you how to be a better parent, but simply share concepts created to stay in the influence game with kids. It's tough to stay relevant in your kids' lives during their adolescent years. Some parents will not be honest about their lack of understanding current culture and social media. Looking the other way is not the solution. We encourage parents to learn to keep up with the culture. We have seen parents lose a child in the hidden realm of social media before they've actually run away. The truth—and the harsh reality—is they were gone long before they actually left home. Our goal is to make sure that does not happen.

TAPPING INTO THE COMMUNITY TO BUILD A CULTURE OF SUCCESS

Parents have provided food, clothing, and shelter—but Dream Building takes parenting to another level. Dream Building for parents is about parents sharing more of themselves by revealing their lives' triumphs, failures, and hopes as an active tool to give children a baseline expectation for them in building their dreams.

LAMARQUÉ'S EXPERIENCE

I was at Panera Bread doing schoolwork one afternoon and during my entire stay I noticed an older woman sitting alone. She was also working on what appeared to be schoolwork. As I got up to leave I decided to ask her what school she attended. She told me she was working on her master's degree. She then asked me what I did for a living.

"I'm a Dream Builder," I stated proudly.

"What's that?" She asked. I then explained to her what a Dream Builder is, she added, "Well, I have a teenage son…" I stopped her and asked if I could finish her statement. "Why sure," she agreed.

"He is going crazy, and he doesn't want to go to college, and you don't know what to do," I stated.

"Yes!" she said. "How did you know?" she asked. I explained to her that this is an epidemic, and while I understood she felt isolated, her situation was more common than she might believe. Parents complain about work and their bosses every day, and then tell their children to take the same path; a path filled with unhappiness. We might want to think about coming home and venting in front of our children about work problems because children make life choices from your example. I told her that she, too, could become a Dream Builder with her child and how to do it. After that conversation I knew parents needed this information.

Questions:
1. Has your family created a mission statement? -----Yes No
2. Does your family have a dream building board hanging in the living room? --------------------Yes No
3. Do you and your children revisit your dream board monthly? --Yes No
4. Do you have a personal vision and does your family know it? --Yes No

---

THE HARD TRUTH

As a parent, I don't have all the answers. There are times when I don't know what to do. This is why I have to have people in my life that I can lean on to help get me through the tough times. I need people who have done what I'm doing; people who can point me in the right direction. I also need people who are in the same place as I am. We can encourage each other not to give up. This is why activating the 7 Levels of Parental Influence with group support is very useful.

PARENT GROUP

The 7 Areas of Parental Influence are areas that you may or may not understand, but if you are willing to commit yourself and willing to be clear and accommodating, you will improve your relationship with your child—even if you already have a great relationship. The group support is where the power lies. There is freedom in knowing you are not alone and that your child is not the only one making poor choices. Having the wisdom—or skill—to love and support them through their process of growing into their purpose is important.

Questions:
1. Have you ever allowed others to support and guide you?
2. Have you supported and guided others?
3. Are you willing to learn more?
4. Have you ever said "I don't know what to do?"

DREAM BUILDERS UNIVERSITY'S
SEVEN AREAS OF PARENTAL INFLUENCE

1. Confidence

Building confidence in our children must be done. When a child has the opportunity to reason with parents and share ideas, it builds lifelong confidence, negotiating skills, and the ability to communicate in a critical manner for life. While pursuing their career, applying for college, or an internship, they will need the following traits: confidence to effectively make eye contact, good oral communication skills, and have a winning presence. Schools water the seeds, but planting the foundation is done at home. Problem based learning and critical thinking is talked about a lot in schools today as something that can be taught but I am not sure if that is true. It is something that we must experience from the time we are young and gain confidence in our personal ability to come up with valid solutions. The smile on a child's face when they begin to realize that their ideas bring value to the world is immeasurable. Over time, confidence will flourish and they will become rock solid in their convictions.

When you begin to unleash this level of potential in your children you must be willing to deal with their lack of wisdom as well. They may get out of place with you and others at times but then it's our job to be able to use the teachable moment to expound the context of their strong nature. If you miss the opportunity to teach this lesson, things might get out of hand. If you do teach the lesson it would look like a nicely trimmed yard where things are in the correct place. If you do not teach the lesson it could look like a yard that has been overrun with weeds. The reality is simple. They are going to grow up either way—just like the grass—but they can grow up trained or wild. Your choice.

Beware: do not let people who are educated with false humility steal your child's confidence.

In schools all over the country, we have insecure adults who do not know how to take a challenge from students. If they are not skilled to coach with wisdom, they steal your child's thunder. You have to hold them accountable. There is a right and a wrong way to do so. And it will always be a work in progress, depending on the teacher who has them for that year. Every year I go through this with my nine-year-old son. He is strong-willed and confident in what he does. At the beginning of the year, I make sure I invest the time in helping him adjust and give his instructors a clear understanding of his heart and our values as a family.

Questions:
1. Do you believe you have created a culture of confidence for your family?
2. When your children display confidence can it be taken as disrespect?

---

2. Creativity

Allowing creativity to flow is a skill. From the way children dress—within reason—to the design of their room. Allowing children to progressively make decisions in the home builds confidence in their creative flow. Research shows that stress kills the flow of creativity. Stress, strife, confusion, and contention have to be intentionally replaced with loving words and actions. When children feel loved and nurtured, they blossom, their creativity flows, and they become more comfortable taking the necessary risks to build their dreams.

The key is to get out of the way sometimes. I have found through my reading and experience that this happens on a several levels. The first is for the parents to get out of the way. What I am implying is if parents would let children take controlled risks in the home they will gain confidence in their creative flow and continue to build new and exciting things that bring value to the world. From playing years of sports at a very high level, I've learned that it is important to recognize that the really great players have had coaches that allow them the freedom to take risks to attempt those great plays. Coaches create the space in which players are confident, creative, and bold. In the home it's the same thing. Parents have to coach in this manner. For me it was difficult at first with my children but I had to put myself last. I listen to other people around me and particularly older people. I have heard so many people talk about what they have done differently with their children. I want to limit that conversation as much as possible. When I become a hindrance to my children because of fear and my lack of wisdom and understanding – that is a problem. The challenge was not *can they become better kids?* but *can I become a better coach in the home?* With a blended family of eight it was—and still is—the largest challenge in my life. But I continue to look it in the face every day with hope and faith.

Parents have to do some things that may make them vulnerable with their children. By doing so, children can see the creative bug flow from the top. Parents that still dream lead the way. Their children see the process that opens the door to opportunity and can imitate the likeness of their parents. As parents we must show fortitude in our desire to paint our own life portrait. The best creativity I have seen shows up in the end because of an unwavering attitude. When our best has not been good enough and we have had to dig deeper, walk longer, and stay up later, we move the universe in our favor and unlock the keys to a breakthrough. In this space our kids learn what it looks like, feels like, and they hear the joyous conversation that comes from these moments.

Question:
Do your children truly have liberty to be creative at home?

---

3. Connectivity

As a parent, making the connection with your child is important. If you do not make the connection, you have given away your ability to affect them. Without this ability you are not credible. If you're not credible, your words do not have power. Leadership is influence and a parent can lose influence due to personal blunders or cultural biases that are downloaded into their child. If they go away from the right life philosophy things can get tough. Life says they will take a few hard knocks from that point on but it is our prayer and hope that they will remember the lessons we instill in them. Through it all we don't give up and we actively wait for the opportunity to support encourage and inspire them to realize their full potential. The culture is impacting them, their thoughts, their decisions, and their actions. It's also important that you take the time to make consistent daily connections with your child. Listening to the funny, boring, exciting, sad, embarrassing, or upsetting events that happen throughout the day can make these connections. When they get older they will see how childlike they were but they will also understand the willingness of their parents to take time to listen and show genuine concern. These connections can't be scheduled. They show up randomly. Are you ready to make the connection?

When you see parents who have that connection with their children you may see it and think wow. I have been that parent thinking wow. Due to the nature of a blended family, I was not there to be a part of some of my children's foundational years where those connections are made. My eleven-year-old daughter sits on my lap and hugs me all day but my older daughters do not. Do they not love me as much as the one that has lived with me her entire life? I have thought long and hard about this and I recently came to a conclusion on this matter. They love me just as much but they did not grow up sitting on my lap. They did not grow up with hugs and kisses from me. They come from an *"unintended family"* and it will take some time for me to develop that bond. The hard part is waiting. I want them to know how much their daddy loves them now. I want them to be free to hang on me as much as they want. I have to remember that they did not plan this. They do not want to hurt their father but they have only lived with me for three years now. I had to commit to the process of showing them love and affection as a father should. Even if they do not show it the way I or their sister does. The key is when they do take the risk to be vulnerable with me I have to receive it and embrace it. Then maybe it will become the norm. Making the connection with our children is one of the most important things in our lives. If you are like me and your kids come from a broken family or "unintended family" you can't control all of the variables, but you can be persistent in the love you show them. It is my hope for you as I hope for myself that they will feel the love and allow you to get a little closer. I promise you it will not be easy and it will take intentional effort.

Questions:
1. Do you think you have the skills to connect? If not, what are you willing to do to figure it out?
2. Would you ask your child how you can make a better connection with them for clarity?
3. When was the last time your child cried on your shoulder?

---

4. Trust

The hardest thing on earth to earn is trust. The easiest thing on earth to lose is trust. Trust is earned, not given. If you say one thing and do another, your children will not trust you. This is paramount. For example, father/daughter dates are a sore subject for me because I don't always do them. I'll say I'm going to do it once a month but then I often find a way to get busy. The result of my lack of attention to detail with my girls smacked me in the face one day. My youngest daughter asked my wife to take her to the store and get a shirt for school. My wife said "ask daddy." My daughter said "I don't want to ask him because he doesn't keep his word." Bam! "He doesn't take us on our father/daughter dates when he says he will." Ouch! My daughter didn't trust me anymore. She came to that conclusion before she was ten years old. I don't want to beat myself up with this issue, but I have to be honest and commit to keeping my word so in time my children will trust what I say. They don't understand how complicated things can get and they should not have to, because as a father, I should make time for them. I have had this talk with my girls and reaffirmed my love and commitment to my time with them. They forgave me.

The best character coaches are our children. My wife and I are open and honest with them when we make mistakes. We do not aspire for them to put us on a pedestal. We desire to be examples of a good life lived by facing and overcoming problems and concerns with truth and passion. They will view us as human, non-robotic, and have an applicable understanding of overcoming life's issues. I am committed to building that trust in their lives. My commitment with my character development will naturally build trust with my children and all other relationships. They will all agree that I am consistent and worthy of their trust. Depending on your belief system, this can vary. But the universal principal that does not change in this variable is that we have to prove ourselves worthy of anyone's trust—and yes—our children are included in that.

I know this is tough to swallow. I've shared my family's perspective on this matter in such a detailed way because I want you to know that we often miss the mark. We believe perfection is not being perfect, but possessing true humility—and knowing when to apologize—is. Even though we are guaranteed to miss the mark, being open and honest is the best policy. Your children can get an audible and visual example of true humility in life. I have learned that God's grace will flow through my children and onto us when they say: I forgive you mom or dad. At that moment I am a child in the presence of the King of the Universe. My children get to experience that mercy as well and can duplicate the process. Again, trust is earned and not given. Are you willing to work for it? Not work outwardly but work from the inside out. Change your perspective, eat a little more humble pie, and love your children enough to allow them to see you desperate for mercy just like they are when they miss the mark. When I can see sincerity and a fortified heart, it moves me. I can say I trust you. Our children are the same way.

Questions:
1. Have you ever lost trust from your children and had to earn it again?
2. On a scale of 1-10 (10 being the best) how would you score your trust level with your children?

---

5. Interest

Are you at the ball game or the play? Being genuinely excited about what your children are doing counts. At sports games I find kids constantly looking up for affirmation from parents to only find mom or dad texting or on Facebook. The parent never knew their child looked up for support. If you don't show interest in your child's activities, they will lose interest in going to school and doing homework because they think you don't care. When others begin to show attention—like when the group at school called the "gang" shows support—things can get difficult. What if they like something you don't? Are you willing to go and support them anyway? Genuine interest moves mountains. I have a friend whose son does not play sports but is the co-chair of the high school booster club. He also has his own company mowing grass and is a Nerd. My friend would love for her son to be the star football player but that isn't his thing. She embraced him as the kid who can fix lawn mowers and cut grass. She encouraged him and supported him. Then her payoff came.

"Mom, I am a nerd," he said.

"A nerd?" she replied.

"Yes—and I am a cool nerd," he said.

When she told me the story, I could hear her smile through the phone. She is proud of him and he is proud of himself. I see him now pretty regularly and his business is growing and he is developing into a bit of an entrepreneur. Saying encouraging phrases like "I'm proud of you," "you'll get them next time," or "we'll get through this together," can go a long way. Our words paint the picture of hope for our children at times when they can't see it. A parent's interest is silently calling out to the deeper purpose of their child when they don't yet believe in it.

In the spring you can see flowers blooming even though it is cold and dark at night. In the morning you can see the flowers that were open during the day closed up in the cold of the night. Our kids are the same. The more sun we give them, the more they blossom. I hope you do not think I don't understand the challenges of families. I know sometimes work frustrations, marital frustrations, and life frustrations can put us in the wrong frame of mind. According to "Love and Respect" author Dr. Emerson Eggerichs, these times are collectively known as the crazy cycle in a marriage study. During the crazy cycle, we can get very selfish and lose sight of the big picture; I do it by losing myself in large projects under the guise of my purpose of when I am serving God. I never thought about it like this, but it is a pretty manipulative way to do things on my terms. This excuse was okay because my wife and kids would not argue with my living my purpose—or with God. What I've just described is just one of the subconscious tricks we use to disarm others who can hold us accountable.

To improve my ability to stay centered in this area I have to open myself up to rebuking from my wife, friends, business partners, and children. I have to be open to accountability on all sides. One of the best phone calls I make is to my t-shirt printer. I follow up about an order and he asks, "How are ya buddy?" I answer quickly with "great!" He then says, "Keep your family first, LaMarqué." When the business and all the people are gone, your family is still there. They are the most important.

Please surround yourself with people who can hold you accountable.

Questions:
1. What are the top three ways you show interest in your child?
2. What do you think will happen when you get good at showing interest?

---

6. Acceptance

When everything falls apart, does your child still feel accepted? When they make choices that you don't approve of, do they feel accepted? Do they feel like they are still loved regardless of their mistakes? Remember that all disagreements are not with the person, but with the ideas that guide the behavior. When it falls apart, we have to get to the bottom of the ideas driving the action. Accepting your child doesn't mean that you condone improper behavior. You can be firm with correction and still let them know you love them.

When they are young they are not wise enough to understand, but when they get older they will be thankful for their upbringing. Instead, give unconditional love and acceptance to the child while exposing the poor ideas. I have discovered in this situation that I'm the person who needs to do the growing. Yes, me. They are going to make bad choices and attempt to pull the wool over my eyes but I have to grow and mature in order to not take it personally. They are children and teens that are trying to do what they see in society. The natural assumption is it must not be too bad if everyone is doing it. I would like to expose and confront the poor ideas so they can learn to recognize and confront the negative influences that can take them off course. This is very important. Taking time to do this forces a parent to take on the role of a coach. *No child wakes up and says I want to be the mess up in the family.* When they make poor choices and we respond, they react to us and then make further assumptions based upon what we do as parents.

The coaching conversation is needed because it gives the parent time to share some intimate moments in their life when they made some similar mistakes and share the results of those choices. In turn, your child will be a little more open to sharing their struggles with you. You can then facilitate the growth process. Sometimes they just need to bump their heads and get a hug. Acceptance can either pull them into the fold or push them away, and when they are pushed away the results are not good. They often turn elsewhere to try to get acceptance—acceptance that they are longing to get from you. They join gangs, or get the crazy boyfriend or girlfriend, etc.

Questions:
1. When your child is not making good choices how do you show you still love them and hold them accountable?
2. How do you balance the accountability with acceptance and love?

---

7. Legacy

Your legacy will be the sum of all the decisions you've made. It really ties into your dream board activity and family vision statement. When I think about my legacy, I am forced to think of what I would die for. What do I want to give to my family and community so badly that I would risk my life to do it? How many lives can you impact with the choices you make? How do you serve your community? If you were to take your last breath now, what hopes, dreams, and passions will you have left behind? I believe this is very relevant and will take precise intentional effort to produce. While we embrace these noble ideas, our personal transformation will be wrapped up in it. Our children will see the process and can confidently declare, "My DREAMS are possible; my parents have paid the price and given me access to unlimited opportunities."

A lot of people do not like to talk about this topic for a few reasons. Either they are scared to die or they did not live their life on purpose and don't want to face it. You can attempt to avoid the conversation but one day you will die and someone else will get to write your legacy based upon what you decided. I do not like that idea. I hope I do not make this seem easy because it is not. It's like riding a bull out the gates at the rodeo. In life we have so many turns and twists every day that we take our eyes off the prize. When this happens, we have to recognize it and get back on track. When the time comes for us to move on from this earth, we want to make sure that we have left a legacy that is worthy. I would love to see you empty all of your hopes and dreams out now. Please don't take them to the grave and rob your family and humanity of them.

Questions:
1. What would your legacy be if you died today?
2. What do you want your legacy to be for your family, community and friends?

ACTIVITIES:

Building a Dream/Vision Board

1. Gather materials. You can either use magazines or image websites. If you choose to use magazines, you should use different types, covering all the topics that you are interested in. You can also use documents that you collect from a particular university or from your work. Altogether, you want to get images that remind you of your goals and ambitions—images which get you motivated.

2. Purchase a board. A magnet board or a large blank painting canvas that is pre-strung on a timber frame, and paper glue. These are inexpensive and available at local art stores (a good size is 1m x 1.5m).

3. Search for images. Go through each magazine and cut out any random pictures that appeal to you. Allow your mind to wander and follow your instinct. Find bright, colorful images that make you feel inspired, ambitious, or fantastic. Try to minimize the words that you cut out. Images are more powerful. Some ideas include: nice houses, cars, flowers, landmarks, fitness models, power words (love, hope, hard-work, fashion, etc.), or clouds.

4. Cut out and place images. Make sure you do this neatly, placing them thoughtfully on your board.

5. Place the dream board. Put it beside your bed or in your office – somewhere you can look at it at least twice a day for about five minutes. Enjoy the images, enjoy your work, and imagine yourself leading the life that is on your dream board.

6. You will notice in the following 12 months that you are starting to achieve some of the dreams you have stuck on your board.

Family Mission Statement

Parents lead the way by drafting a written copy of what you desire to be your personal legacy. This will be the foundation upon which your children build. The children should also write theirs—and as a group—bring all of them together so you can create a document based upon your family mission. In this document will be ideas, principles, and values you champion as a family. Everyone has to be on the same page.

Family Fun Night

On this night each person in the family should be able to pick what they would like to do for fun at least once a month. This will support the building of strong family relationships and everyone will realize what is important to each individual in the family.

Have a "Fave Five"
(Two Elders and Three Dream Team Families)

Two Elders: This list will consist of two people who are older than you who can impart wisdom and grace from their life experiences to enrich yours. Through this relationship you have to establish clear communication standards for honesty and tough talk. It's funny how brutally honest gray-haired people can be—they tell it like it is. If you do not feel comfortable being this vulnerable that is fine. Do as much as you can. If you are comfortable opening up to one family and one elder then start there.

Three Dream Team Families: These families are at the same level of parenting as you, and you only reveal what you feel comfortable sharing. These people are your cheerleaders and you are theirs. Operating like this is helpful because you don't feel alone. You know that other parents are going through things just like you are. You are encouraging them in areas in which you have a greater understanding and they do the same for you. And finally, the children feel the support and love and Build Their Dreams!

Family Character Checklist

Compassion (vs. Indifference)
Investing whatever is necessary to heal the hurts of others.

To practice Compassion, I will...
- ☐ Stop to help
- ☐ Listen when others want to talk
- ☐ Give of my resources to help those in need
- ☐ Look for lasting solutions
- ☐ Comfort others without regard to race, gender, faith, age, or nationality

Diligence (vs. Slothfulness)
Focusing my energy on the work at hand.

To practice Diligence, I will...
- ☐ Finish my projects
- ☐ Do a job right
- ☐ Follow instructions
- ☐ Concentrate on my work
- ☐ Not be lazy

Forgiveness (vs. Bitterness)
Clearing the record of those who have wronged me and not holding a grudge.

To practice Forgiveness, I will...
- ☐ Be quick to forgive
- ☐ Not cover up my own wrongs but will be quick to ask for forgiveness
- ☐ Not seek revenge
- ☐ Respond kindly to those who hurt me
- ☐ Not take up offenses against others

27

Faith (vs. Presumption)
Confidence that actions rooted in good character will yield the best outcome, even when I cannot see how.

To practice Faith, I will...
- ☐ Expect the best
- ☐ Make right choices based on principles of character rather than the whims of circumstance
- ☐ Believe the truth and reject a lie
- ☐ Not take things for granted
- ☐ Trust those who have proven character

Self-control (vs. Self-indulgence)
Rejecting wrong desires and doing what is right.

To practice Self-Control, I will...
- ☐ Not act impulsively
- ☐ Not equate desires with rights
- ☐ Set my own limits
- ☐ Walk away from things that are not right

Published by: Dream Builders University Press

Edited By: Desiré Bennett

Contact:
www.dreambuildersuniversity.com
Facebook:
www.facebook.com/DreamBuildingForParents

Follow Us on Twitter:
@dreambuilderu
@lamarqueward
@lkobie

www.ingramcontent.com/pod-product-compliance
Lightning Source LLC
LaVergne TN
LVHW010024070426
835508LV00001B/44